Wakefield Press

T0358110

Black Swans

Peter Lloyd was born in the English Midlands and emigrated to Australia in the late 1970s. Most of his active working life has been dedicated to providing housing for the under-privileged. He lives in the Adelaide Hills and is married with two children. Peter has had work published in Australia, Canada, the United States and France.

black
Swans

Peter Lloyd

Wakefield Press

Wakefield Press
Box 2266
Kent Town
South Australia 5071

First published 1997

Typeset by Clinton Ellicott, Adelaide
Printed and bound by Hyde Park Press, Adelaide

National Library of Australia
Cataloguing-in-publication entry

Lloyd, Peter, 1930–
Black Swans.

ISBN 1 86254 398 4.

I. Title

A821.3

To R.G.C.M.
Their families and friends

Contents

Mandarin oranges

So cold,
so refreshing:

a small mound of iced-mandarins in a china bowl;

each time she opens her mouth, he spoons
a morsel between her lips

& smiles;

as light fades into fluting pink beyond the windows,
Orion starts to blaze:

meanwhile, the old woman's jaws go on working
little shreds of fruit;

when he wipes her front —

that is heaven too.

The black swans

He keeps his days in paperbags
& feeds them to the birds:

hand, stick, bone, eye,

as the stick needs the hand, the bone needs the eye —

but his cough tears them apart . . .

they skitter up like little red kisses from the grass,
among his boots; they circle his head, twittering,

while the ghosts of last night's guitar-playing,
all-electric boys & girls suddenly vanish

on gold heels by sky-diving into the sun.

Apricot mornings like this among the trees in the park,
send the old man mad with desire —

but his cough drives them apart

coming up into his throat warm & soft as phlegm;

his stick taps   while a small breeze, stretched tight,
scatters the dahlia heads which sway like red

penicillin lampshades lit from underneath, frail as human skin.

when the old man coughs again,
filling his mouth —

black swans emerge through the white mist
shrouding the lake

hissing like co-conspirators.

Autumn

Don't spit,
        blow! my mother said

over the birthday cake:
                & so it happened,

years later, the door opened again,
another woman came into the bedroom with the face of a stranger,
weeping & lamenting,

naked & carrying a piece of icing on a plate:

autumn leaves blew from her eyes

& there was winter-paint
in her hair: I swear!   thick winter-paint.

And it only took one breath.

Parlour Trick

The man lay there:

footsteps
came

& went: then more footsteps,
there were voices:

someone, in a sunset-pink with trees in it, drew a sheet over his face.

The room filled; a man sat down & crossed his ankles.
Another lit a cigarette
& there was talk.

His wife brought coffee.

And all evening, all the next day,
through the greetings, the talk, the neighbours,
the coffee in little cups

& his sons,

the man lay there on his back & said nothing.

But he did it so beautifully.

The blanks

It's the way they keep slipping on down past —
& I can't stop them,

leaves, dead trees, old photographs,

past the window — silhouettes,
no one, even our children,
will remember;

sometimes, in a garden mist, a whole annex will
melt away like a fresco in
bad paint

by damping & peeling off, mouths
silently opening —

but it's the way nothing turns in passing, waves
or hesitates   as if the holes in the grass

had already grown used to it:

it's the utter emptiness

of the blanks undulating formlessly on the mantelpiece
which drape themselves round the clock

before sliding down the walls & across
the floor,

dumb mouths snapping at the clouds.

Pastourelle

There's a row of pink houses
& a row of white houses:
>   I live here.

There is also a red sun
& a blue sky.

This morning, a green bus drove up the Avenue. I added this to
the list of primary colours in my immediate environment.

Italianate women descended: they were carrying blue/white striped
or yellow/brown parcels. Most wore black.

I append these facts also to my list:
the children were olive-skinned: the women, too,

but with certain blemishes which did/not contain hairs.

This morning, early, I heard my neighbour retching, coughed-over, his stick
dropped on the ground as he reached into his throat,
deep & with one finger hoiking,

so that the whole piece came away smoothly.

Sitting behind curtains, I have to remind myself occasionally
of what it's like to be completely well.

Afternoons, I prefer long slow walks through the concrete suburbs, studying
the effects of those interior forces which are thrust (as Sabbrin observed)
remorselessly through the whole geometrical solid on which we stand:

these, viewed at distance, emerge as parallelograms & diagonal lines —
in turn, become divisible into more triangles   & so on.

This is where the organic energies & speculations in Monet go so
          much further.

All afternoon, I was thinking about Monet — when I saw a wonderful thing:
suddenly, it was raining: sun & rain mingled so that the long
shining liquid in each drop became a slim goldfish

slanting down, each one with an open mouth & a wriggling translucent tail;
these beautiful creatures swam through the air, an enormous shoal
of descensions glittering & suiciding on the pavement.

Across the road, a supermarket, brilliantly white as icing,
tall as Everest, was framed perfectly by a rainbow
                                        stretching from suburb
                                                to suburb.

Three times, my feet vanished among green puddles.

Carer

Was changed at six this morning. This is the second time
in the bath, holding onto the bar;

her hand goes between his legs, into the crack of his bottom,
water swishes as his penis erects
                            & he turns his face towards
her her her her

& his mouth, slackening to vowels, wah-wah-wahs,
                                  tongue lolls pleasurably

he splashes his feet —

at dwarf-fortyish, dumb but sharp (as they say)
she's used to this,
blows a wisp
of hair from her eyes,

folding him in the big towel
as she brings him from the bath

& holds him close
close
close,

the child-wet of his beard against her neck,
                          against her cheek,

as she towels him down.

And he fingers her eyelids, prises her lips & tongue.

When he leans his face against her face,
you can see he's in love with her though he's never spoken
in twenty years.

Sister.
Brother.

The rain

Evening of still breaths / chemotherapy at
sunset & steroids — a verandah

rocked by a wooden chair: almost chalk-ninety,
bone moves her through an old house, a misfit
of waterclocks, gross tumours

in fern time / or

through glass embroidered door knobs, shawls
& cameoed rose gardens

laid out with golden nutmegs & silver stones
in a row . . .

Sitting up all night,

being sometimes woken by sheet lightning over towards
the citrus groves where the road

merges on the retina for an instant above a town glaring
out of actually hot flesh & real eyes

among the lemon smells of the glutinously green leaves . . .

sometimes, during the thunder, half in terror, half
ecstatic, she cries (still rocking on the verandah)

'. . . to die now!   at this moment. . .!'

as the lightning flickers, printing with dry glass
the black glimmer of chimneys against the sky.

Under the trees and beside her, the house moves,
daguerrotypes staring from round frames, the few
flowers mummified as claws

in Waterford glass yellowing on a tablecloth:

'. . . to die now . . .' she whispers,

the roof reverberating again as it passes trembling
through the thunder in the iron

& she leans forward feeling for the first intimation
under her feet, that gentle tearing at the grass,
at the foundations

(in the darkness, any moment now)

that will take the house in the dry storm like a leaf
whirling upwards over the electric lemon groves —

staringly huge eyed as she moves with it also
where it is going —

breath by breath towards the rain . . .

The greeting

Smiles from the sky,
smiles from the house when the gate clicks open —

& from the garden, the Schneewittchen roses,
Papa Meiland in red cloaks,
                              bowing:

the showy delphs., top of a big crabapple tree putting an arm
around her shoulders . . .

        (shakily, yellow-toothed
                  after her months in hospital, her first time home)

old beards of iris,
the lipsticks & polka-dots,
the amateurish hairdos, a small shed waving its shadow,

all the tiger-stripes & dianthus, the wobbly high heels —

with everyone talking & laughing, everyone
trying to make themselves heard:
                              grabbing hold of her case, kissing
                              her cheek.

A broken spade on the path,
a watering can.

Then a hubbub of questions & answers

— almost deafened by the Wichuraiana, besieged by voices
    as she leans down, touches, pats a tow-head, cuddles, nods to,
    shakes her own head —

& might seem even a little t-taller now than when she arrived,

starting to l-lose
the worst of her stammer,
                    but trying to take it easy, speak slowly,
                    smiling at everyone through her long yellow teeth,

blowing unexpected kisses:

f-family.

The curse

in the night silence of a street
i heard the mother of millions swear she'd come again —

    as the hump on her back moved
    as the legs moved at angles to the stick

                & her long coat flapped —

i heard the mother of millions
scream that she'd return

no longer the sweeper of black floors, the child bride
in a hovel where semen leaked through stained walls

    but next time around, half rat   half dog
    sister to the harpy   daughter of the lean midwife

called at night with her basket of knives to the big houses
on the hill of the bastards who'd refused
                her children suck:

    before they dragged her away
    i heard her scream she'd rather be shit

three crows flew out of her mouth

                one for the father
                one for the son
                one for the holy ghost.

once in an eerie nimbus of light
candles glittered at her throat

i heard an old woman curse her life

wind howled through the altar

                    her head was screwed around
                    her tongue nailed to the tabernacle

                                        as if it belonged

in the morning

there was a half eaten sentence still lying on the ground.

The well-dressed city

Mother dresses like this —
                              and father

he dresses like this:

                    the children do not like their hair
                    being combed. But mother will wash
                    behind their ears; she will see that
                    their shoes are brightly polished —

and that Janet has a broad blue ribbon in her hair.

Father — he walks like this:

                    and mother

she walks like this
                    as hippity-hippity-hippity they walk
                    right across the clean white city. No-
                    body talks because today is not a talk-
                    ing day. The policeman smiles to see

them go.   The sun is high.   The sky is blue. In
the well-dressed city on a no-talking day . . .

in their smart black-silver monogrammed and domed
high helmets — and their scarlet boots —

                                        why!

even the policemen are dressed to kill.

In that neighbourhood

In that neighbourhood

among the Rolls Royces of silence
& Heidelburg paintings like a hanging mist between the trees —

this evening, purple & a few flowers,
I saw the aged parents
                    of the newly-rich

shuffling first
one step
& then another

as they went out lone, singly, stooping every now & then
with little poo-buckets & brushes

to sweep up their own footprints, each one as they occured
by roadside, on grass,

beside the bushes,
under the trees:

& each one as they happened again,
returning, each old person stooping, bending,

fingers stiff & softly rheumatic tidying up their own shadows

& quietly putting them into purse or bag at the bottom of driveways

so that each step taken from now on
was in the absolute silence of a ghost.

Grandly the doors closed behind.

Wrecker's morning

— is a tangle of belly-hair, Doberman-scratched, listening
at the chainfence, listening to
the wrecker's yard,

      listening to first-light sprayed Dumpster-grey
      between two sheds:

is a dog among oil-puddles piled Ferrari-red, rust-green
at the manbeast interface —

      suddenly hurls itself at echoes, cloud-buildings,
      & falls back, barking

at coo-names whistled
blocks-back through wet mists on the road:

      is a dog among lost traffic lights
      & mag-wheels at the end of its chain-skid

launching itself bodily & fanged through whatever smashed windscreens,
mud, hidden planets at the manbeast interface

      to hang black

      ears two-pokered

at the steel gates & absolutely rigid with it.

Old Fenian

A hook nose
the sunbitten maks of a Demetrios

and still fugitive —
maybe with the same price on his head
as fifty years ago
the night he slipped out of Cork,
rain and mist beading his cap:

sometime revolutionary, old Fenian, now continents away and here,

& God knows no catholic,

but the mark still on him
in the tongue and lilt
like blood is thicker than water, the music
of Saor Eire, Clonmel and Brugha,
all the old Gaelic names in a big wind
bashing through from the Atlantic

to streak window-rain into Galway

& bounce and smithereen
among the sough of kith and greenswell on Slieve Mis,
over Errigal.

Barefoot and madder, a whiffle of clouds flowing over the peaks,

an Irish sunset come down from the hills,

or an old spade thrust to its own helvings among weather:

glitter of lanterns, night, wet grass,
distant voices snatching beside a wall,
turfcutter's smoke.

Like an old print behind dusty glass wiped with his sleeve

& ineradicable upon him
as bowed legs, scaffolding,
the creased trenches of a lifetime
                                        spent dizzying with the sun on his hod
among the tilt-ladder sway,
whistle and hardhat of his world

        (though should he ever go back
         when not even his own hands know)

But nothing's new to his century: who, at eighty, wandering might
as the old do

through so many coombes, grass-haunts,
drip-drip of earthworks,
fogs rolling over green bracken in his mind,

slowly duffering up
to whatever memories

while filling his pipe.

> Kerins who hung,
> Pearse, Plunkett, O'Connel,
> Dev's Party,
> McGaughey starved dead, the Post Office siege,
> the Falls Road, Yeats, O'Neil,
> the Penal Laws
>
> & the dum-dum-dum of the Orange Drum . . .

scrapings from the torn quick of a bloody fingernail scratched into a cell wall.

Whose names bitter-sweet take his tongue in theirs
        (& with no stone turning between bawn & gleaning

should you meet him at some dusk)

his chalk-spined saunter stiffened to a labourer's load
of bricks & black flint, weightlifter's shoulders
& a pair of broken cheekbones.

Maybe it's the soft vowels
walking his own shadow home

                that leave no skyline between you & moon.

But the mark is on him —

how like a man on a strange road
in a strange time

he puts his feet down, each step a careful one:

the way his coat flaps in the dark,
the unreadable tilt of his left shoulder,

the other arm still weighed down by that invisible gun.

Glitz

Moonpeople are always
distances

away;

so very softly, quietly,
anonymously, facelessly invisible,

oil & a latchkey silently turning a rented lock,
dead post cramming a letterbox,

wild dandelion heads:

who leave no footprints in the garden,
never arrive before night,
stand, eat by candlelight,

always shh!

the children of moonpeople never cry: they walk on tiptoe, very lightly
like this

    (with large dark eyes)

Until heat,
without sheets, one summer night from across the way
arrives with tyre-squeals, footfalls on concrete & loud voices,

loud hectoring voices at 3 a.m.;

headlights from a debt-collector's car which swivel fast,
settle hard & brilliant on the ceiling:

then hear them far-away through a listening breath
over the pound of fists on doors,
                                & the rise & fall of dust-motes —

moths, as they wake suddenly   dazzle & burr,
the large sounds of soft wings banging hopelessly against black glass,

crawling hurriedly up the walls.

By morning will have vanished

leaving just this little light glitz
of sequin dust hardly noticeable on your hands,

               nothing on the bare boards.

Always & far away

It's all of a piece in the dark:

a gasp behind some broken window,
shouts
        shouts

up abandoned liftshafts.

The sound of running feet.

Then silence.

On a third flight up, she relaxes
her grip on his shoulder —

as instanced by lipshadow & sex-poem with mask,
or scarred dresser & figdance,
blue apple on neon dish.

The moment is over.

A box of tissues with vaseline & ghost-building
slowly circles a wasteland in starlight
of deserted cars.

& the woman opens her legs again.
The bed moves.

Sunset from the Park

About his own business in the city, the dwarf comes & goes:

> people step aside because he's misshapen,
> so people are afraid & they step aside;
>
> his old hunch moves like a worm,
> he mouths indistinguishable cyphers,
> he's a dero's coat of unknowns tied with string,
> his chin is filthy with spittle —
>
> some say he's mad: not defective just   but mad:

      though once, back of tenements, night & rain across wastelands,
I head his voice shrieking, heartbroken among street lights,
crying as if it was something there he'd come to now
& never seen before:

backwards & forwards he rocked front of the church,
backwards & forwards on the pavement, his coat over his head in the rain,

as he wept in the rain,
while his voice rose in the rain & he wept.

And all his life was excrement.

That was then.

Now see his wonderment.

Is radiance. He shines. Is dazzling with wet gums
as he drags the sunset from the Park:
                                    leaves, dirt, trees, bushes by their roots

up the street
& through the traffic lights without pausing

so that not even Picasso

would have known what to do
with those massed pinks, winged eyes of children, waterfalls
& blank faces
          in the clouds.

And is all his small crippled heaven,
          flowers & lake waters, the big sunset on his back:

when he sees the girl
in her new yellow hat

looking in the shop window — suddenly, middle of the street, he turns
& darts towards her open-mouthed with his three black-stump teeth shining,

his tongue lolls further towards ground as if tasting metaphors:

as he tries to take her hand
& they step around each other.

I mean when it's so completely ineradicable as happiness.

Pieta

Here, a man & his woman are joined together
in a Saturday afternoon of love —

is landlordland, back of the Poison Factory, corner
of Odessa St, a neighbourhood behind invisible barbed wires
& the million-drifting faces

of pollen-immigrants astray among Greeks calling, Italians
scrawling fish-menus Calimari-grey on the windows
of their world:

& two ordinary people are making love.

When Meditarranean people die owning landlordland, their grieving families
erect memories in Carrara & Siena marble with white gloves
& emerald angels whose nippleless breasts

& massive wings beat forever in the cemetery by plumping
the thighs of the dead.

Mine is a simple Pieta

of a Christus in a bedsit   naked   who becomes a child without metaphor:

he is a man in her arms:
he is a man like a man at the end of cement corridors, among tatty carpets
& lying across a mattress:

he is a man like a horse,
like a horse with empty eyes:

he is a man after love
lying exhausted among cartshafts & tangled sheets —

whose rib-cage expands powerfully, whose diaphragm sucks air,
whose nostrils' hairs plume work
into the enormous volume & smooth-skin of his breathing:

one hand   lies on her leg   sleeps there perfectly still

& those great sweat-drops
on his face

Michelangelo never carved

When she opens her eyes
                         she's in pure stone with wings folded,

two butterflies are slowly sipping
in the middle of each iris.

If she had milk to give him
from her breasts

she'd give it.

A saggar for the five towns

King China with snakeheads

crawling down Main St emitting SSSSSS-vowels,
splintered teeth, waving arms in the smoke
which danced before cinders & flame

                                (before the sphincters of locomotives,
before Jazz with its hair on fire)

& Wedgwood who went mad with Visions of Alchemy,
shaking gigantic leg-chains & howling with trumpets
behind electric Hallowe'en masks as he leapt
with backburners in his hands to light the underbelly of the clouds:

or a potter's curse
gobbed sizzling on a furnace door —

a billowing spillage of phosgene & turmeric smoke, with slab-sided
factories gone fogged for mile   after mile   of potbanks
into whistling straw & cobbles.

This is where the soot fell,
                           the soot fell,

but still the 19 hundreds by my birthday in the clock,

                                      sudden as a boot
                                      through a Turner canvas,

big-snorting through double gates,
come the great horses, the shire-horses, crack
of a carter's whip, to lurch, humpback the load, hooves & froth-bite,
six to a team that crash & clash dray-haul clouds

& crockery across the rim-wheel & rut-bed of the world. Splinters

& pale shards I still pick
from lost margins in moonlit candlegrease,
from clinker & earthenware under vanished hovels,

with words like urn, jug, saggar & kiln —

smashed epochs & jasper dumped into a marl-hole, filled.

Or set perfect among Bacchus & nymphs
in long quiet rooms, glass cases, polished floors:

pieces remote, unbreathed on,
fingerlessly delicate

& luminously white as ricepaper fluttering over a black lagoon

in a museum   museum
of echoes

echoes.

Free-speak

who, on the morning of due execution,

also gave voice to your many pissholes of sorrows & your dreams
    when he asked of the prisoner before him
                         — what is truth? —

these million essays on the human state,
these scribblings in the city at dead of night:

                     on the cosseted façades, acres
of marble, astraglass, stainless-steel, on the ecstasy
of neon-lit silences, in brick, on miles of concrete
spires, white towers, domes; on the fabulous frontages
down easy-street, on the prestige fabrics of bankers,
moneylenders, wheelerdealers & the purveyors of glass-
tipped ceegars, diamond tiaras & private yachts

— likewise on the handy notepad of the massifs which
house multi-national corporations, marijuana growers,
pimps, tipsters, thieves, barristers, MPs, entrepreneurs:

on public buildings, communal lavatories, on
the crenellated dreamboxes in which the verbum divinae
of authority is dispensed in the name of politics & justice:

how the police would love to cop this lot —

the masked potato using red paint
the mysterious gloved-hand which zaps on the aerosol
the dirty mirror with false eyelashes

giggling in the dark as it cartwheels away back to the slums
    & leaves big plastic footprints in the road.

                                          O graffiti!

blank wall on which nothing yet is written!

may your people be my people.

let your witness
be my witness,

brother.

<u>Level 50 psych.</u>

He is at the 50th level as lift purrs, stop —
& he enters the offices to explain;

indeed, everyone is very kind, eliciting slowly only
the practically essential from the details, which, like

yesterday, today & the day before, have enmeshed themselves
around what he really has to say. Smiles

bump gently against the ceiling like small balloons:
but there are no stethoscopes here. The sound

is only of filters through which waste-air is drawn:
the same antiseptic cleanliness that makes more important now

all that which he has memorised & reiterated before —
thus turning himself again into that sharp instrument

he does not recognise as being himself. As the silence stretches
out, fingers are steepled patiently, a mouth pursed into

vagueness floats behind a bowl of flowers on the desk.
He is sitting by the window at this 50th level up,

the sky is violet, small cottonwool clouds seem to be nudging
the ediface. Certainly, he feels in this quietness that he

could linger here — even, perhaps, be happy too. As the howls
of the street fade, suddenly he finds himself weeping.

The red underwear

Beautiful red underwear she has on today, walking through the Park
in her brand-new underwear!

That's why the lake bows prettily & looks so different: under her coat
for all-weathers, her woollen skirt, Scottish with a shining pin —

is a secret.

The world doesn't know.
The flowers know. The lake knows.

If she sprawls this morning & her jaw lolls, it's because she's feeling good:
each step heaves & leans on callipers, her hips roll, the crutches go.
Massively hunched shoulders muscle & bunch.

                                    The flowers nod: is Spring.
Bearded irises, reflecting coloured sun in their incredibly round
& think prescription glasses,

fix her with buckteeth smiles. Daffodils wave.

Tall trees wave by the lake. The sky waves its stump.

And what a beautiful day for walking over grass with a pair of crutches:

with each step as it brings her now in her enormous coat, moon-faced
through the Parklands towards the Sheltered Workshops in her life:

but the elastic cuts, chafes: around her waist,
her new red underwear, with each leg thrown out into an arc,

her terrible breasts swinging with effort
go every way:

with each black boot
plonked down, grinding grass —

two crutches go robotlike into distance, go wrong, grimace prodigiously,
start again towards horizons & are absolutely remorseless in preserving
the oneness & identity of being she,
her crippled self:

                   of getting there   of getting her there,

& yard by yard is hauled.   Through air.   Her crutches haul her;   her legs
                                                     two legs.

And arrives.
She arrives: sweating, red-faced, her first sentence, gabbled,
            falls on the grass. Her tongue flops.
                                  Gets mixed up again.
                                  Tugs at her underwear.

But she has arrived.
People take her indoors.

Happening

Lookt!

had hardly,
had almost

lookt,

then lookt again —

a sunset speck hurled in colour

> through the stuff of heaven   ablaze!
> through the stuff of earth   ablaze!

bulleting the air:

a million pink sheets on fire & drifting,
an exploding pizza-parlour lit by a neon-glass floor,

with legs straight,

long wingless plummet vibrating the membranes flattened in
her face: solo venturer daring the zero of incandescence, ultimate
explorer at the last frontiers

in the absolute totality of self:

with arms rigid
with body rigid
with feet rigid   like an arrow   letting the air take her weight.

Her mouth open for the pavement!

then straight into her own sun.

A single splash
like Icarus.

Childless couple

Every autumn now   more bits slough off:
first the heels, white flakes

snowing dandruff, his shoes, his socks.

Then whole square centimetres are caught up & ripped
off in barbed wire, she finds

everywhere. It is that time of year he becomes
shockingly white lipped.

Recently, undressing for bed, a complete sheet peeled
off like plastic from his belly

suddenly blew over his head.

For a moment, she saw him lurch like frankenstein.

Now blue harpic flashes lightning from odd corners,
old happenings grow delicately as new skins —

in the orchard with its strange orange light, like two
sisters, they were always naked.

Hips, breasts plump   smiling   their hands

rehearsing marriage. Her marriage & her marriage.

while very gently oiling each other again. Very tenderly
& possessively. Because they knew that this

would go on forever. Because in the orchard there could
be no end to the orange light.

Hand in hand they walked under trees. Over the unending grass.

When it was dead   she said   '. . . take it away!'

All down the street, 'For Sale!' boards rattled
in the wind. & people were digging.

People were always burying things:

tight lipped
4 a.m. finds her in blue moonlight

still scrubbing the house
picking up old pieces of skin

heart machines screeching from every corner.

The protagonists

Like two steel needles in cold blood,
his silence
her silence

like two hostile silences clashing against each other
with implaccable energy:

like two steel knitting needles
jabbing at each other's throat

above the awful silence of a polished floor:

like two swordsmen in fencing masks

his silence
her silence

like two thin pointed steel knitting needles
among the domesticity of stitches

going for the jugular:

twin kamikaze
two virulences skewered in from the wrist,

violence upon violence

thrust through a skein of wool

noiselessly glittering in the air,
endlessly circling her fingertips:

like two long steel knitting needles,
his silence
her silence

in their absolute fight to the death
in their terrible fight to the finish

as the garment grows longer.

The Caller

all Saturday night
has been bending over the bed   messing about

under the old woman's nightdress in the dark:

daylight finds
new blood on his nails
his tools

tall & thin   whistling a tune, he scrubs off
in the kitchen
then departs
the garden gate swings in the sun

later, she weeps,
finding smears of her own dirt on the sheets,
half-blind, hobbling
on her stick, she makes tea —
she'd know him anywhere

what she calls him,
a name unlike any other name,
ordinary, extraordinary enough,
but leaves the curtains drawn,
her door on the latch for Monday
neighbours:

& though such things obligatory are not,
                     but for appearance-sake,
        whoever in a white or blue coat comes
            officially stripping back the sheets,

will find some old towels wadded under her —

a clean nightdress pulled over her hips —

     & enough small money folded
     as makes a funeral.

The mask

As skin aborts   flesh
crinkles   each blister spitting its
pinprick of yellowy
fizz:

the scratches dry & scab this thin black-berry-brown.

Full-length, the man, fiery-scarlet, lies naked on the bed
while his self-image goes on tearing
at his body again   there's a mask over his head, a cripple's boot
on his foot;

his imaginary fingernails are curved
& crowsize;

the mask could be the massive
head of an animal
moving blindly in its stall, hearing its long chain clink;

propped on the bed with its pink duvet,
the invisible boot is disgusting

  (but, as the mirror says — why should I
  feel differently in myself to all these things
  than I have been before:

  above all, since nothing changes, what could be less
  in self-hate now
      not to make it so)

When the naked man moves backward into himself, he goes
into memory like a third eye splitting open
in his forehead   a hard mottle

discoloured as iodine splashed among old waterstains, a spillage
of rust-green in a cold Victorian bathroom
& the smell of Jeye's Fluid in the air

                              (& down the years)

a wet sop on caked lint —

piercing as high-pitched screams
of a child held down & still quivering as the bandages are unwound.

Sound of music

The 'La donna e mobile'
                                of the wife-beater
cleaning his fist off under the kitchen tap;

the low melodious whistle of the child-molester
        following the toddler behind the toilets
                in the park;

the hum of the pervert kerb-cruising at midnight,
        lights from a police-car flashing on his cheekbones, a coiled whip
            on the seat,

looking for the divine act of faith with a ten-year-old
        and the profile of a Madonna:

as notes from a shining trumpet fly up to meet it . . .

or a jazz pianist
links the rhythm-section with his front men,
weaving into & away from the melody line with slick turns
squeezing & dragging —

so the grand sweep of a coda comes singing through the massed waves of
    an orchestra

when the blurred fingers of a sweating maestro
        suddenly appear over the tumult on the neck of a polished Stradivarius

in the long, sweet & piercing tremolo
of one note being

held   held   held . . .

This is a moment in the life of an artist which is the pure machinery of self.

After that, only silence is unendurable.

The twenty-thousand-dollar bed

Years ago, where she arrived like a skydiver almost
degutting concrete — at the last moment,

braking to the amnesiac's dead-fall through white, a thin
skin sighing out articulations.

This is room 426, & by morning 5 a.m., the nuns are
busy (where a mezzotint of the pope

faces an alcove in which the virgin with folded hands also
floats among blue plastic flowers)

After the bag-wastes have been removed, the sheets are
stripped, a switch activates —

so elevating the bed
as the steel clamps move across:

& this dank, twenty-year-old female
vegatable with shaved blond hair

    (a trunk only)

is lifted naked & dangling tubes — on this apparatus
which is now separated into two parts

by cantilever rods, the upper & the lower:

    (although she feels, can't feel anything, they insist)

but seems at this moment of lifting, an almost-shriek,

                high & thin as a child,

as she is washed,
as she is given to the sponge & towelled.

Meanwhile, the gears rotate, the bed tracks & swivels,
in which the patient is held & turned

through ninety degrees as the shadow, also distorted
& held aloft in clamps, revolves

like some obscene eucharist among the scentless flowers.

To the accompaniment of the high-pitched keening,
where the nuns are spreading laundered sheets:

— it is the morning offering in room 426

— as the first prayer of the day before mass

— just as the moon is going down.

The perfectionist

The right hand holds the cane:

through the window, it is summer   people sitting, walking
over the lawn   the sound of children laughing.

Whenever the left hand moves, it is beaten back.

As seen through the same window   but from outside
both the right hand & the left seem vaguely, almost impossibly

attached to the outline of the artist seated before
the piano in the room.

Sunlight falls blindingly in a mirror.

Whenever the left hand moves towards the keyboard, the right
hand moves: the tip of the cane blurs, slashes —

until stunned   helplessly inert, the hand falls away again.
Observe the hand lying on the carpet

at the end of that oddly twisted & distended arm: that with
each new thrashing it is becoming more of an appendage,

more like a lump of flesh.

Old cuts, bruises   the joints of the fingers so swollen into
each other that the oedema bulges over the nailbeds

themselves blackened & chipped.

Meanwhile, however, very softly, quietly   very tirelessly
beautiful   the third & fourth hands of the artist play on

    (whenever the left hand moves, it is beaten back:
     the cane swings & smashes mercilessly)

For hour after hour —

afternoon moving through the windows into dark   as people
depart   & the first stars appear over the trees —

the figure plays on   with the terrible perfection
of its own appassionatas rippling & silvering in the mirrors.

As the artist listens to his own hands.

As moonlight fills his mouth.

Sale!

Amid the roar & hubbub of the store — this
is the salesman's desk: I sit.
He sits. Among other such papers here,
this is the document.

He looks. I look. But with which hand take
& sign it? The one dangling
at my side, hangs withered in its sleeve:
the other six, wrapped in pockets,

have no fingers today. Or with which eye
read the finer print — I
have one that porpoises crazily behind its
glass of snow-green-arctic,

the other is covered by a whitish growth.

Amid the roar & hubbub of the store is where
I sit. Is where the salesman sits.
This is his desk. Though an older man, he is
still a flexibones:

his stomach rests upon a bole where grey-silk
baboons sit all afternoon
before they vanish up his arms — a single gold
magician's tooth

is also wired for sound. Then because I smile,
he smiles. The flash! He nods.
I nod. Tropic ferns begin to sway: between my
feet, a silver orchid

opens up. I smile. He smiles. We nod. They nod.
        '. . . is this a pen?' I ask
as a single flower drops upon the desk. And because
pens also explode — I write myself

quickly into the sudden ecstasy of ten thousand
colours drifting through a sphere:
then a flight of parakeets swooping & whistling
round the chandelier.

How now and goodly

— Sir,

and what a rude & redly
frumps this old clown's nose,

this weird water pudge in a wight's welkin

diddering over its own dottle:

old paunchy, pork crutch, pisspot's barrel, a booze beaver
at the ceildh channerin' over a chaudron,

the devil's left tit waving a vergissmeinicht;

nose above all other noses lit by bulbs —

fool's danegun,
doughty dint,
green snot blower,

a corbie on the corse craking & squeaking,

some mischance, cran o' the face, brinded, braid,
a laith lazybeds & ilka nostril as it huntly goes.

Is it a joke

      when its own hame harps & carps?

There's nary a near: if we dight on it we do,
if we don't we're damned.

And that's the end of it, mirror.

Odd birth

thought it was a poem
>(O the gurgle & the guggle of my heart's transparencies,
>>blue dungarees flapping about my ribs)

& barfly drunk, legs gone, singing there
like an old time revelation priest

might have baptised it

'if thou be human: in the name of the father, son & holy ghost'

but she screamed

its shape odd, blurred
spat, hopped, danced, mewed fur

spun over the floor, heads dangling
& clawed open, smashed & splintered

left these tracks to the orchard

its birth cord

two of the heads dead, still wet
the others staring up at the sky

on its legs, reaching for the sun, claws, breeze, clouds. it was smiling.

it stood there smiling

as i blew it away

loaded again
& fired twice

still drunk went to fetch some sacks.

Soapie

That last episode on TV —

                     we missed: the set banged,
                     blue electricity shot past us in the dark:

suddenly, rushed forward from the screen again,
a faceful of knives, two tongues twisting & writhing:

everlikely we became junkies
when we discovered love;

people undressed
& didn't get dressed,

people undressed & never got dressed again:

by then we were in Dallas: the world tilted, we fell:
that night in Dynasty,

                no wonder you cried & we were in heaven too.

Ah!   Dallas!   Dallas!   Southern as Comfort.   Texas!   faraway as
    the moon:

all the perfumes of treacheries & oil wells:

    what crystal attendants, furious veils, Egyptian masks, bouquets
    of roses skinned alive & screaming in a golden vase: what silken
    deformities, snick-snick of scissors, lies, tears, crucifixions,
    dooms drowning in bottles, gape of red wombs, deaths, crotchless
    white knickers, semen stains & splashes of saliva on the sheets:

    Wave after wave: the bands playing, crowds cheering: everyone singing
      Dixie:

    territory of the quick billion, confetti of murders & capped teeth,
    boutiques crammed with giant cocks, glass uvulas, prodigiously wet tits.

Ah!   Superbitch!   almost you odoured us of the dead that night,
                      a big breastful of worms, endlessly writhing
                      worms, writhing endlessly in colour

& something that slipped & smelled vaguely of dogshit underfoot.

To zonk us out: like sleepwalkers dreaming
as we went to bed, lay there listening to the rain all night

& never closed an eye.

But in the morning it was still pelting money.

Sons & lovers

he stands there naked while she makes him.

    she makes him after her own image. like some
    crazy horse her legs on poles going over the mountain,
    gathering leaves & cuckoo spit, bits she plucks from
    the top of stockings, snippets of her wedding
    gown, a pike of old 78s.

        when his voice occurs, she hears it
        like a wind dragging an orchard up by its roots

    & she works faster, copying lines from Shelley, buying
    racks of new clothes, shirts from Tennessee. her fingers
    click like metronomes. her needles goes in & out.

she wishes clouds & they happen.
she stamps her foot & landscapes appear.
everything comes true.

even years later
struggling from bed

she can hardly believe it — but her skeleton rushes past
    one breast tied in a pink knot, the other
                          leaking milk

down the stairs its high heels making stickying sounds

    while the noise of his boots walking through the sky
gets louder & louder. they climb the corners
        of buildings. push fences over.

splash through back yard pools.

at the door she opens her arms

the wind blows. moonlight howls over the carpet. under the black shadow
of his hat, galvo crashes & reverberates.

lip to lip they will cling for hours together like this
softly telling the same story

whispering the same lies.

Invisible

Seven enormous men with beards
sitting at a table:

six huge men in a restaurant sitting elbow to elbow round a table
& their father sitting at the head of the table:

beside him is an empty chair.

Listening, I think they are talking in Russian or Croat,
maybe Lithuanian. I think of Murmansk & Siberia,
of reindeer & snow, of the great winds sighing at the top of the world.

Their plates are pushed back: voices rise:
six young giants sitting shoulder to shoulder — & their father —

their father with three gold teeth

& their mother in the empty chair beside him,
very small & wearing a black hat,

who smiles & nods her head,
who sits there completely invisible.

As she nods her head & watches the birthday cake, all its candles
blown out. Seven tremendous men,
their fourteen feet crowding together under the table,

emptying the bottles, lighting cigars, as they laugh & lean back,
lean forward among their lives, among the glasses —

& their mother in an empty chair at the head of the table,

who says nothing: only her eyes & her smile go backwards & forwards,
from face to face, hands, mouths of each one,

so going round the table,
her sons & her sons' faces

& between her sons' faces,
the other faces going round the table & beside each son:

each wife
who is also completely invisible.

The red dress

This young girl's walking
& all the sweet buds of her

     (as mirrors are to streets, clouds, etc.)

she's walking through Spain in her mother's red dress,
everything smooth & sewnup tight behind:

as the wind rocks,
as she goes under the entrance of her red dress —

so the dance is to mirrors, streets, the cafe, the old men playing cards.

     Pow!   as she puts one borrowed high-heel shoe down.

     Pow!   a second deadshot

as she points her instruments
& the old men look up from their cards

     (with that young man studiously reading on a bench under
       the pepperines)

but as a dance is to clouds, streets, town, pigeons strutting,
the cobbled plaza, etc.,

as everyone looks up —

comes a third passionate shot.

     Suddenly, there's a poem hanging in the air.

Ole!

with a flick
of her mother's fingers

& the red dress vanishes into the sun.

Discarding her nightdress

Discarding her nightdress,
she becomes an etude by Schumann:

some shaven darks do straddle her legs

& there is a moon on the roof
under the soft palps of her rib-cage.

I can feel Schostokovitch's great drums beating:
when she lies beside me I am listening to Chopin.

At breakfast   she laughs into my mouth,
                 I laugh into hers.

All day, we hold hands.

We become Braque & Monet: a single line drawn across the world
establishes a series of diagonal charges;

when we exchange faces in the grass,
we become indistinguishable as successive states of movement

trailing apricot dream-modes through Lhote's Trees.

Butterflies flex their wings: all afternoon, huge architectures
move slowly over our heads towards the sea.

Once, at night,
parted for a moment by traffic lights

— we panicked —

& then ran towards each other
through the dark

like two unfinished poems
waiting for the last line.

The Italian connection

When one comes   (one)
hoeing around the family tree in golden soil —

are many purples of flowers very pompadour-sweet.

When two come   (two)
the old people,

dinner-smells drift among bean-rows: plates clash musically,
they gather knives & forks;

when three come, there are more:
when three come, there are six come

bringing many beautiful heads of children, the carved
heads of children,
                    & where to speak Italian is an armful of roses —

like a dozen in dark,
three moons,
two stars

& a huge woven basket of sweet grapes.

All day, white tablecloths & green vines wind lazily down the street.

And long until evening comes   evening
& the old people come,

soft voices watering lawns:
lente, lente   signori e signore — in soft slippers,

darkness & a star among rooftops —

or simply climb up
into the family tree

& vanish forever.

But the voices remain.

The wedding party

His mother
& what she remembers:

                her son walking up the aisle like a marionette

trailing black electrical wires
& invisible red sparks

while the bride
came to occupy a space
in a silent bone-forest of tall, gaunt lilies
with tinted cheeks,

a white veil floating
as the air-conditioning roared.

Or the mother of the groom —
dead neon in stone

& brocade
under a blue picture-hat,
making an anonymous gene-donation to another family

she sat contrariwise to   nevertheless   & in a front pew
eating perfect dirt:

benind her,
more thin seas of taffeta & silk,

black ties & lame:

came later

pictures

in May sunshine
outside church

& a few cool centres whorled delicately round
alabaster flowers in a bouquet of fragile roses

— found her hours later at the reception, fifty-ish, with a knife
behind a half-eaten cake,

blank-faced & waving to someone on the
outskirts of the party,

also in a blue hat & ringed by enemies.

A time of growing

Was it laughter from the garden

or a cold wind —
a draught blowing from the bottom of the world:

suddenly, a door opened
in space,

the children stepped through

& vanished.

An invisible dark shadow passed between house & sun.

It was as if a handful of molecules
silently flowed out to form elsewhere —

had dispersed between-fingers,

& you were left holding the subtlety of water.
That's it.

The subtlety of water.

Diary

Of smokey glass?
A leaf?

Or a small cloud fallen out in winter
& left to weather among the grass?

Rereading an old diary, he found it there.

Light streaked within light
with the vague lightness of nothing,
but still light:

it lay there with its eyes closed,
no breath, no stir.

He touched it with his finger:
no movement:

he touched it again & felt nothing.

So taking it very gently, very quietly,
he placed it between
two pages

& went on
reading again.

What else can you do with a dead soul?

Autumn mist

Of all the leaves tonight,
the sad leaves rustling my feet,

I gather three —

> its own signature an oak tree has been working on for months,
> a small Cezanne with a splintered frame
> & a piece of sheet-music by Satie with blue oblongs & green squares, I'll

> take home through the mist someday & play like a candle against
> the dark.

How beautiful & remote they are,
quiet in my hand, waiting for the Millenium.

Old hips lie in their wicks of grass. All their lanterns are out.

And I have no place to go.

I will wait here in the park as for a woman, in the dark-listening,
mist-moving white & blue distances of the town lights

where the words of dead poets carpet thickly as dead leaves underfoot:

I will wait here for the moon to rise through
the treetops of my tongue.

And I won't move.

Flock

Strange how far-away other graves were
that day it rained:
                    weeks later,

coming back, the mounds were just two low mounds,
fathers & mothers of the other graves seemed so much closer,

had moved closer, circled, moved in —
        almost as if knowing,
                as if sensing,

& when your gravestones came,
their simple granite
                    erected,

seemed, last seen years ago —

grey-backed, lost, found, lost again in the mist, among the old prayers
in the rain clay-soiled
                        or just standing there like gulls

among others, the flock, the elders, the one-eyed
in a marsh waiting for daylight to begin.

And nothing to do with you.

When a new funeral came,

they whirred, wings flapped & whirred,
circling the ground

raucously.

The kiss

Are very duvet-soft
& pillow-propped,

elderly Mr & Mrs in bed tonight,

asleep, not asleep,
dreaming & half-dreaming,
touching but not touching

    while the glove drifts past their windowsill —

londonromewashingtonsydneybeijing
chinarussianorwayaustraliafrancevanuatumoldaviacyprus:

perhaps if he touched her in Paris,

she would die in Berlin
& go straight to heaven:

maybe she would become a vine,
a tremendous vine with trellises, bosses, curlicues & knots of interwoven
pubic hair, nests & leaves in the moonlight,

under whose foaming branches
he might lie forever, stunned,

if he touched her.

If she touched him —

suppose she made a pink anemone with her wrinkled mouth, turned
& slid her hand between his legs —

who knows

what deaths & which soft words
skewed in fine lines & poetry

might not wake
& follow them
quietly as a baby with a melted foot
in the same electric field,
                              go vaguely tiptoe & whisper from room to room:

or one bladder being full,
the other bladder being full,

struggling into dressing gowns —

simply gesture & vanish.

Gesture once & then vanish.

Legend

the tribes went north
        hopping like kangaroos
                flying like emus

they carried firesticks, water

but the hoovR men were there before
        chivvying   swooping

if the tribes turned their heads   the hoovR men were there
      if they turned the other way
           jet-trails flashed through the sky

     when the hoovR men beckoned
                 rogue lawnmowers chattered through the mirage
        leaving watered strips of grass behind

when they waved long sensual fingers from the clouds
      the jaws of the womenfolk clacked like ducks
          & fell forward into front-loaders

all night dishwashers
    winged south

K beaters whirred in the dark

& fires flickered
    as the tribes crept closer

but the tracks went on multiplying

they circled the camps
    closed the exits

in the morning when the hoovR men & the last stars
        or the last stars & the hoovR men
                        suddenly blew their trumpets . . .

herds of wild television sets stampeded through the bush.

The howl

Mornings when a desert stirs, dinosaur bones   put on new kneecaps,
walk on stilts: swales & skeletons dance with horizons:

when a desert waves an orange scarf
& suddenly starts to roll — flies from Flyland go for miles before it
through the wheatfields, blowing fly-trumpets,
playing fly-flutes
& beating fly-drums.

Any fly, gazing in hot midday at a desert on the move, sees through
     the beautiful
stained-glass windows of its eyes   senses its own destiny:

its face wrinkles to a gape,

the black tongue unrolls & moistens death with its coming:

the sun hisses & becomes a lizard,
the moon is infested with beetles.

When a desert goes on the move, it simply pulls off
its clothes & starts walking towards it.

It holds its balls & howls.

Towns drop dead.

South of Frome

Curios!   you pull them out like photographs again —
              a broken pram, a shrivelled kangaroo hide

& galvo cracking in the sun, spread-eagled
        as it moves closer to red earth;

you pull them out:
                        at a distance
                                    stick-figures   emus
                      trailing wires & a crazy plumbing,

or, closer to,
        a man lurching down Main St
        under a flap of black skin,

a tall hat clutching a green bottle.

If he is merely the dry whispering of molecules
        sliding over each other
                                (if he has no face)

what are the ants dragging
from under the shadow of his brim:

when he climbs in at hot midday through the broken window,
                                            on what thing
liquescent & faecal are the flies
            congregating under that pile of soiled newspaper?

But you pull them out:

>among the bottles,
>a naked foot protruding from the pepperines,
>a row of stone dogs,
>two carved eagles in the sky —

&, at the last moment,

>>a waitress,
>>who, when you suddenly appear by the
>>>coffee machine,

starts to pedal away furiously
on a dwarf wheel

fixed under her long purple batik dress,
>round & round the tables

>>(with light whistling from her nipples)

amazed, as she shoots through to the kitchen
>waving a dirty rag.

Dawn underfoot

dawn underfoot & stop suddenly —
shrieks feathers at the last moment, rises
& peels off through a shattered pane of sky,

long grey-thrawn wings, some goosneck stretched in flight,

sick cries
circling a thick cloud
in mist, bad light,

as it planes slowly, wheels to follow our footsteps
over the mangroves
towards the sea,

an old lament whose origins outstare the pricking of our necks:

how now, uneasily looking up, turn back the evil eye,
avert the clocks

or cure the coughing sickness in the sun?

until a sudden sea-scud, out-white & bootfall-silent blankets all . . .

which, with oil-silks wet, chilled,
later we share with the small souls of sticks
& a black fire which smokes
back of a dune,

hunkering, wipe
our plates with bread.

little humps in the pan
                              sweet on the tongue

six eggs.